£16.50

# LAWRENCE WEAVER
## 1876–1930
### an annotated bibliography

# LAWRENCE WEAVER
## 1876–1930
## an annotated bibliography

by
LAWRENCE
TREVELYAN WEAVER
with a contribution by Patrick Nuttgens

YORK
INCH'S BOOKS
1989

First published 1989
This edition limited to 500 copies

Inch's Books
3 St Paul's Square
York YO2 4BD, England
© Lawrence T Weaver, 1989
'Lawrence Weaver: Architectural
Writer'. © Patrick Nuttgens, 1989

ISBN 0 9514277 0 9

Generous financial assistance from *Country Life*,
London is acknowledged in the production
of this book.

Printed and bound by
SMITH SETTLE
Ilkley Road, Otley, West Yorkshire LS21 3JP.

To Lawrence Purcell Weaver
and Tobias Rushton Weaver

# CONTENTS

# PREFACE

Lawrence Weaver is best remembered as an architectural writer. From unlikely beginnings and unconventional training he achieved a unique authority to write about what may be called the interface between architecture and the worlds of industry and commerce. His active years were a period of great change in building style, materials and methods. Starting as a commercial traveller in architectural hardware, he soon became a manager with a firm of builders and engineers. Gradually he turned to architectural journalism, which culminated in his architectural editorship of *Country Life*. Public service in World War I led to his involvement in the foundation of the National Institute of Agricultural Botany in Cambridge, and to his appointment as Director-General of United Kingdom Exhibits for the British Empire Exhibition of 1924-1925.

Throughout his career Weaver was in contact with many of the leading architects of his day, including Edwin Lutyens, Robert Lorimer, Percy Morley Horder and Clough Williams-Ellis. The last, who with other young architects owed much to Lawrence Weaver's patronage and counsel, wrote a memoir of his friend which remains the fullest account of his life.

This bibliography lists my grandfather's published works chronologically and comprises his books, some of them recently reissued, his articles, essays, lectures and guides. I have tried to include all he wrote for *Country Life, The Architectural Review, The Journal of the Royal Institute of British Architects, The Architects' Journal, The Burlington Magazine, The Antiquaries Journal* and *The Builder*. He also contributed to a number of lesser known architectural and trade journals, many of which have ceased publication. I have not included published letters or notices unless they had something substantial to say. Some unsigned articles may have been missed, particularly in *Country Life*, where during his period as architectural editor his authorship is variously indicated by his name, initials, simply W, or not at all.

Two bound copies of Weaver's early articles on leadwork are in the library of the Royal Institute of British Architects, and volumes containing articles he wrote for the series 'Country Homes, Gardens, Old & New' and 'Lesser Country Houses of Today & Yesterday' may be found in the archives of *Country Life*. As far as I know he kept no record of his publications. I believe that this bibliography contains all the major books and articles that Weaver wrote.

In compiling this bibliography I have been helped greatly by Susan Glen. *Country Life* gave free access to their library and archives, and lent generous financial support. It is a source of pleasure to include an essay by Patrick Nuttgens assessing Weaver's contribution to architectural writing. I was encouraged to write this book by Peter Inch and Janette Ray who persuaded me that Lawrence Weaver represented an important figure in the history of early twentieth century architecture. I hope that his work may be of some value to those who believe this to be so. To all those who have helped me with the production of this book I am grateful.

Cambridge 1988

# LAWRENCE WEAVER
## A Biographical Sketch

### Early Life

Lawrence Weaver was born in Bristol in 1876, at about the time when the Queen Anne style was beginning its revival. The only child of parents who separated soon after his birth, he owed his upbringing, and education at Clifton College, to the determination of his mother, who taught the piano and bred Pekinese to support them both. In later life he ascribed his own success to the example of her 'grit, concentration and natural ability'. On leaving school at seventeen his initial plan to become a dentist was abandoned when an older relative helped him to get a position with the Bristol architectural practice of a certain Youlton, about whom little is known. He seems to have been more of a sales entrepreneur than designer. In his second job, with the Birmingham firm of Lockerbie & Wilkinson, as what he liked to call 'ironmonger's bagman', and later with Robert MacAlpine & Sons in London, he compiled catalogues of architectural ironwork which included such rainwater goods as eaves, gutters, down-pipes and heads.

In the process of learning about the history of these items, particularly those made of lead, he created a portfolio of photographs and notes. Published first as articles in *Country Life* and other journals, these formed the basis of his first book *English Leadwork, its Art and History*. With a working knowledge of building techniques and materials, familiarity with the manufacture of household equipment, proven success in journalism, and an enthusiasm for architecture and its allied arts, in 1910 at the age of 33, Weaver was appointed architectural editor of *Country Life*.

### Country Life Magazine

Under his editorship there appeared a series of articles on the architecture and restoration of country houses throughout the British Isles *(Lesser Country Houses of Today and Yesterday)* as well as books by him on the design, construction and repair of small country houses and cottages and, in collaboration with Gertrude Jekyll, their gardens. He contributed over eighty articles to the already established series *Country Homes, Gardens, Old and New* and edited a number of supplements on architecture including one devoted to the work of Sir Robert Lorimer (1913). *Country Life* ran competitions for the design of houses and gardens which were judged by Weaver and his colleagues. The competitions stimulated other illustrated articles followed by informed criticism and comment. Together these articles and books about domestic architecture before the Great War constitute an authoritative record by a man who understood the interrelation between design, construction and materials through the firsthand experience of his earlier working years. Weaver may justly be included among those who prompted Walter Runciman to describe *Country Life* in 1913 as 'the keeper of the architectural conscience of the nation'.

Although Weaver was never an architect (he claimed he could not draw), his knowledge and understanding of the subject are shown in his biography of Sir Christopher Wren, and his edited facsimile of John Shute's *The First and Chief Groundes of Architecture,* the first substantial treatise on the subject published in England. His practical interest in the architect's profession is illustrated by his detailed collection of the accounts for the building of Wren's London churches, and his obtaining for the Royal Institute of British Architects an interleaved copy of Wren's *Parentalia.*

With his articles in *Country Life* as its foundation, Weaver's literary output from 1910 to war's end ranged widely in period, subject and scale from accounts of mediaeval dwellings, to sixteenth century buildings and large contemporary country houses. His study of the greatest living exponent of the latter, Sir Edwin Lutyens, contributed to an early recognition of this architect's achievement. In his preface to *Houses and Gardens by E. L. Lutyens* he claimed to have described and illustrated the work of nearly two hundred architects in the pages of *Country Life.* In spite of a familiarity with scores of great country houses throughout the British Isles, Weaver retained a taste for the simple, together with concern for the design of homes for the working man. This commitment was later to find expression in public service and charitable works in the field of housing. Many of his books of this period were reprinted or enlarged and updated by him in the course of time. To these architectural books he added such varied works as a history of the Royal Scots Regiment (he edited a series of *Country Life* military histories which included a companion volume on the Oxfordshire and Buckinghamshire Light Infantry by a fellow Old Cliftonian, Sir Henry Newbolt), and *Memorials and Monuments*, in part an appeal for higher standards of memorial design. A later booklet describing Robert Lorimer's Scottish National War Memorial at Edinburgh Castle expressed the realisation of these hopes.

### The Great War

Weaver gave up his post as Architectural Editor of *Country Life* in 1916 to do wartime service with the anti-aircraft corps of the Royal Naval Volunteer Reserve (though he continued as a major contributor to the magazine all his life). He was soon transferred to the newly formed Food Production Department, whose head Sir Arthur (later Lord) Lee quickly made him Controller of Supplies. This phase of his life opened up new areas of activity and especially provided the administrative experience which, with his other qualifications, would lead to his appointment as director of the United Kingdom section of the British Empire Exhibition in 1924. As civil servant Weaver became in 1918 Commercial Secretary to the Board of Agriculture, and in 1920 Second Secretary of the newly formed Ministry of Agriculture and Director General of the Land and Supplies Department within it, posts which he held until 1922. His powerful organising abilities were brought to bear upon the pressing problems of food supply generated by the recent war and its aftermath. Using his expertise in architecture and planning, and through his appointment of Clough Williams-Ellis as the first full-time architect to the Ministry of Agriculture, he initiated projects for the employment on the land of men returning from the war; these featured improved agricultural methods and the utilisation of land and the buildings until then neglected. In response to the postwar rise in the cost of building he encouraged the use of traditional materials like cob and weather boarding, examples of which can be found in the revised editions of *The Country Life Book of Cottages (1919 & 1926)*.

## National Institute of Agricultural Botany

Weaver's wartime experiences suggested to him the need for a single institution to coordinate and direct crop development. To this end he was instrumental in founding the National Institute of Agricultural Botany in Cambridge. The Institute's buildings were designed by his friend Percy Morley Horder and opened by the King and Queen in 1921. Weaver served as its first chairman of council from 1919 to 1924; his portrait by Lewis hangs in the panelled council room above the fine table and chairs, also the creation of the architect. In recognition of his wartime work Weaver was made CBE in 1918; he was elevated to KBE in 1920 for his contribution to postwar resettlement and rehabilitation.

The demands of his work and these appointments did not prevent his finding time for charitable endeavours. These included the foundation of a pottery for the employment of disabled ex-servicemen at Ashtead, Surrey, which produced, among other well designed wares, models of the Lion of Empire, the official symbol of the Wembley Exhibition. He was one of the founding trustees of the Housing Association for Officers' Families in 1921, and of Douglas Haig Memorial Homes in 1929. In these housing activities he saw to it that the dwellings were architecturally well designed with equal attention to their internal furniture and fittings, and external setting. Weaver also became a trustee of Chequers after its bequest to the nation for the use of Prime Ministers, by his old friend Lord Lee of Fareham.

## British Empire Exhibition

Next came a challenge demanding all of Weaver's talents of judgement, taste and organisation. The Wembley Exhibiton of

1924-1925 was planned to show off to the world the diverse achievements of the British Empire, in pavilions representing twenty-five countries of the Empire on a site of 216 acres. Inspired by the fresh continential style of presentation which he had seen at the Munich and Gothenburg exhibitions of 1922 and 1923, Weaver sought to achieve in Britain a new artistic standard with a unified arrangement of displays emphasising quality of exhibits rather than a mere advertisement of wares. To this end he insisted on a uniform lettering on displays; an alphabet based on the Trajan Column inscription was used as guidance for sign writers and adopted officially for the Palace of Industry. His untiring efforts and practical shrewdness of judgement earned him the description of 'National Professor of Commonsense Art'.

With the experience gained at Wembley he set out his views in a major book *Exhibitions and the Arts of Display*; illustrations of many of the British stands were included in it. His reputation took him to America where he visited the 1926 Sesqui-Centennial Exhibition in Philadelphia, and lectured in Pittsburgh and New York. He also took delight, as well as a leading part, in the publication of the *Book of the Queen's Dolls' House*, a record of Edwin Lutyens' exquisite creation for Queen Mary. Shown first in the Palace of Arts, part of the United Kingdom exhibit at Wembley, the dolls' house is now at Windsor Castle.

Weaver's contribution to the Wembley Exhibition marks the summit of his achievements. Upon his considerable experience of the commercial, architectural and administrative worlds, his success as a public figure of the time, as 'liaison officer between Art and Industry' was established. Chairmanships of the General Exhibition Committee of the Advertising Association and of the Architecture Club, were appointments which followed. The Design and Industries Association, whose watchword 'fitness for purpose' could have been his own, also made him their president from 1926 to 1928. As a member of the Royal Commission on Cross River Traffic he pressed for the preservation of Waterloo Bridge. He remained a director of Country Life Ltd. and became a director of an advertising agency, the London Press Exchange. His contributions to scholarship had received earlier recognition with a Fellowship of the Society of Antiquaries and Honarary Associateship of the Royal Institute of British Architects.

## Last Years

When he had just turned fifty and was at the height of his strength his wife Kathleen Purcell, a gifted harpist, died suddenly after nineteen years of devoted marriage. In this difficult time two close friends gave him particular support. Stafford Cripps, whose family took on the care of his two sons, and Bernard Drake, his solicitor, came to his home every week to bind books with him. Another distraction was the extension of his working day. By now he was a personality greatly in demand as a lecturer and an after-dinner speaker. He enjoyed these occasions which allowed him to present his views on a wide range of interrelated subjects. The flavour of his speech can be appreciated from the many pieces that were published, in such places as *The Outlook*, 'a weekly review of politics, reconstruction, literature, drama and art'. In 1928 he married Margaret de Caux and his difficult time appeared to be over. However his relentless drive and excessive hours of work, coupled with insomnia, were taking their toll and early in 1930 he died suddenly of a heart attack at the age of fifty-three.

His memorial service was at the Catholic Apostolic Church in Gordon Square, where he had regularly worshipped and served for many years as a deacon. His involvement with the Irvingite Church, was known only to his closer friends and was outwardly separate from his worldly work. However his faith was undoubtedly a major influence on a character which, in the words of his biographer, combined 'strong religious, puritanical and philanthropic convictions' with enthusiastic and energetic participation in the workaday world.

His obituary in *Country Life,* his literary springboard into later endeavours, made a generous assessment of the breadth of his qualities. Lawrence Weaver was 'rapid in judgement and unhesitant in action . . . with the artist's love of beauty, the zeal of the reformer, the philanthropist's tenderness for his fellow men, the cool and far-seeing efficiency of the business man and the empirical methods of the man of push and go'.

## Sources

C. Williams-Ellis. *Lawrence Weaver*. London: Geoffrey Bles 1933. *Dictionary of National Biography 1922-1930*, entry for Lawrence Weaver by Christopher Hussey. J. Cornforth. *The Search for a Style*. London: André Deutsch 1988.

Obituaries from *The Times*, 11th January, 1930; *The Architects' Journal*, 15th January, 1920; *Architect and Building News*, 17th January, 1930; *Journal of Royal Institute of British Architects*, 15th January, 1930.

Family papers.

# LAWRENCE WEAVER
## Architectural Writer

## By Patrick Nuttgens

Architecture is the most inclusive of all the arts and it is not only an art. It involves many disciplines and is one of the great exercises in synoptic vision; it is the product of many arts and many skills. Writing about architecture is not and never has been simple.

Lawrence Weaver was one of its finest exponents. He was recognised in his day, largely forgotten for some years after his death and then celebrated again as a definitive figure in the annals of architectural writing. In that process his reputation is a mirror of that of the architect he most admired and wrote happily about — Edwin Lutyens, forgotten for twenty years, now recognised again as possibly the greatest architect the country has ever produced.

Weaver had no apprenticeship as a writer and hardly any as an architect. He worked for a short time in an architect's office but soon went off to work as a purveyor of building materials. His first writing was the study and promotion of leadwork; from that specialised subject he widened his scope to writing about houses and land and architecture. Of leadwork he wrote one of his most evocative pieces:

'Among the debts of gratitude which architecture owes to lead, there is none more weighty than its use in roofing. The roof may be said to be the second need of architecture, as the wall is the first. The wall gives privacy, the roof brings protection. The spire is the supreme form of the roof; it is the roof spiritualised. In its relation to the Gothic spirit it has a character all its own. In its essence it is the roof of a tower, but it intends more. It is a constructed symbol of aspiration, and its building is one of the greatest concessions to constructed beauty and symbolism which Gothic art has made.'

Such a blend of practical observation and lofty inspiration remained typical of his writing throughout his career.

What changed his career and established him as a writer was

his contact with *Country Life,* founded by Edward Hudson in 1897. Hudson's first thought for the title of the journal was *Racing Illustrated.* Then he recognised that there was more to country life than racing and it became *Country Life Illustrated.* The series on *Country Homes, Gardens Old and New* started in 1898. Weaver was not the first contributor to that series, but soon after he started writing for the journal in 1905 he became the most authoritative of its architectural writers. He was architectural editor from 1910 to 1916. The articles written and commissioned by him were probably the most influential upon the commissioning of architecture ever published in this country.

His output of articles — not only for *Country Life,* as revealed by this bibliography — is formidable. The books were sometimes based upon the articles, sometimes new. Probably the best are *Small Country Houses* of 1910 and *Houses and Gardens by E L* of 1913 — both many times republished and enlarged.

If Lutyens became the most celebrated of his subjects, it was Lorimer who personified everything Weaver liked most about architecture and was the most profound influence on his judgements. He admired everything Lorimer stood for — the crafts, romantic grandeur and history built into the idea of the buildings. Scotland seemed to bring together the themes he was most moved by and best understood.

About his writing itself, there are two major points that must be made. First, he wrote at what must have been the most wonderful time to encounter architecture and write about it. It was the 'golden age' of the English house, celebrated throughout Europe for a degree of professional perfection and sophistication unknown before and, for the most part, since. For Norman Shaw, Philip Webb and Edwin Lutyens — and for many other national and provincial architects — it was probably the best period for commissions. It was also the best period for building construction and services, for all the components and gadgets that made English domestic architecture supreme.

Weaver perceived that it was the small country house and the cottage — grand, of course, compared with ours — that would be the major contribution of the period, not the huge Victorian pile. Lutyens and Lorimer were supreme at that scale. Weaver's articles, and ultimately the book, established that house as the superlative building type of the time.

Secondly Weaver's writing places him among the most exemplary of architectural writers, with an authority that comes, not from portentousness, but from an unpretentious command of his material and absolute clarity of style. His writing is characterised by that clarity (rare among architectural critics and almost unknown among architects themselves), but also by an unusual analytical precision and by a logical method of presentation that leaves out nothing essential and wastes no time upon words for their own sake.

It may be that his exceptional organising ability, notable especially in his direction of the Wembley Exhibition of 1924, was always there in his writing. He analysed buildings in terms of their history, technology and design. He wrote, without jargon, not for the specialist but for every intelligent person. It was a simplicity of style based upon knowledge of the subject.

On *Gardens for Small Country Houses* he wrote in the first sentences of the Introduction:

'It is upon the right relation of the garden to the house that its value and the enjoyment that is to be derived from it will largely depend. The connection must be intimate, and the access not only convenient but inviting. The house, in the greater number of cases, will stand upon a slight platform, not only because it is better that it should be raised above the ground-level, but also because the making of such a platform is an obvious and convenient way of disposing of the earth or sand excavated for foundations and cellars.'

Of Walter Brierley's house, Bishopbarns, in York he pointed out that it was 'a compendium of domestic comfort and makes for a perfect organisation of domestic affairs.' He recognised the needs of all the participants in the life of a house, especially the servants: 'It would be difficult to devise a plan for the work ing quarters of a house more convenient for their purposes.'

Writing about the work of Edwin Lutyens in the second edition of *Houses and Gardens*, Weaver said, 'He has by one little work — the Cenotaph — made joy in fine architecture a possession of the people. Wholly admirable as it is in its own right, as a piece of austere design, it is much more. It was accepted forthwith by every one gentle and simple, by those who use strange phrases about Art and by those who have never thought of Art in terms of human life, as a perfect expression of the Nation's grief and thankfulness and of its pride in the Glorious Dead.'

In the 1922 Edition of *Small Country Houses of Today* he remarked, with some justification, in the preface: 'When the first edition of Small Country Houses of Today was published in 1910, I did not forsee that it would be the pioneer in a series of five on houses, their equipment and their gardens, which have found favour with the house-loving public through many editions.'

At a time when the houses and other buildings described and analysed by Weaver with such clarity have recovered their reputation and can be seen again as some of the most distinctive and inventive of any period in this country, his writing itself, to anyone who reads it afresh, is a model of presentation. He was described, after his work on the Wembley Exhibition, as 'the national professor of commonsense art.' That would not be a bad description of his writing. But it would miss the analytical power and directness of perception and expression that made him a most singular interpreter of the architecture of his age.

# BIBLIOGRAPHY OF THE WORKS OF
## LAWRENCE WEAVER

# PART 1: BOOKS

## Listed by year of publication

### — 1904 —

*ENGLISH METALWORK*
By W Twopeny (1797-1873)
Foreword by Laurence Binyon
Notes by Lawrence Weaver
Archibald Constable: London, pp 96
This selection of some of Twopeny's architectural drawings shows Weaver's developing interest in architectural metalwork, particularly in lead. It contains reproductions of 93 of William Twopeny's drawings taken from thirteen folios presented to the British Museum in 1874.

### — 1909 —

*ENGLISH LEADWORK: ITS ART AND HISTORY*
By Lawrence Weaver
Batsford: London, pp 257
Lawrence Weaver's first major work is based on articles from *Country Life, The Burlington Magazine, The Architectural Review* and elsewhere. It was published a year before he joined *Country Life*. The book includes chapters on fonts, rain water pipe heads, cisterns, spires, statues and garden ornaments. It is well illustrated with 441 photographs and line drawings and includes a substantial bibliography of earlier publications relating to the history of English leadwork.

### — 1910 —

*SMALL COUNTRY HOUSES OF TODAY*
Edited by Lawrence Weaver
Country Life; G Newnes: London
C Scribner's Sons: New York, pp 222
1911 Reprinted
1912 Second edition
1922 Third edition revised

1983 First edition reissued by Antique Collectors' Club:
Woodbridge
The first, and one of the most successful of Weaver's books to
emerge during his architectural editorship includes articles
from the *Country Life* series 'Lesser Country Houses of Today
and Yesterday'. The 1922 edition contains the work of 16 new
architects. It is a companion volume to *The House and its Equipment* (1911) and *Small Country Houses, their Repair and Enlargement*
(1914), edited by Lawrence Weaver, and *Small Country Houses of
Today* (volume 3 of second series) by RR Phillips (1925).

## ARCHITECTURAL COPYRIGHT
Edited by Lawrence Weaver
Country Life: London, pp 32
This handbook includes a correspondence on the subject from
*Country Life* with three appendices and an introduction by
J W Simpson. Contributors included Lutyens, Voysey &
Lorimer.

## THE ART AND HISTORY OF BRITISH LEADWORK
By Lawrence Weaver
Royal Society of Arts: London, pp 15
The Cantor Lectures, delivered to the Royal Society of Arts in
1910, were published as a pamphlet as well as in the RSA Journal.

## — 1911 —

## THE HOUSE AND ITS EQUIPMENT
Edited by Lawrence Weaver
Country Life; G Newnes: London, pp 212
1912 reprinted
This is a companion volume to *Small Country Houses of Today*
(volume 1, 1910; volume 2, 1919) and *Small Country Houses,
Their Repair and Enlargement* (1914). It contains chapters on
water supply and sewage disposal, the design of grand pianos,
outdoor dining rooms and air gas in the country house. The
editor wrote six chapters, and Gertrude Jekyll wrote 'On Garden
Design Generally'. His chapter on Libraries & Bookcases
includes a history of the care of books, and photographs of
lecturn cases in the Library of Trinity Hall, Cambridge.

## — 1912 —

### GARDENS FOR SMALL COUNTRY HOUSES
By Lawrence Weaver and Gertrude Jekyll
Country Life; G Newnes: London
C Scribner's Sons: New York, pp 260
1913 Second edition revised and enlarged
1914 Third edition, revised
1920 Fourth edition
1924 Fifth edition
1927 Sixth edition
1981 First edition reissued by Antique Collectors' Club:
Woodbridge
1983 First edition reissued by Papermac, Macmillan: London
Gertrude Jekyll wrote frequently for *Country Life* and this is
the largest of the works that arose out of her collaboration with
Lawrence Weaver. It is richly illustrated with plans and photographs and throughout stresses the interrelation of house and
garden. There are chapters on pergolas, gateways, sundials,
seats and statues.

### THE FIRST AND CHIEF
### GROUNDES OF ARCHITECTURE
Facsimile of the first edition by J Shute of 1563 with an intro-
ductory essay by Lawrence Weaver
Country Life: London, pp 80
A folio edition, limited to 1000 copies, of the first major work
on architecture published in England contains reproductions
of Shute's copper plate engravings. John Shute was a 'painter-
stainer' and 'servant unto the Right Honourable Duke of
Northumberland' who sent him to Italy 'to confer with the
doinges of the skilful maisters in Architectur, and also to view
such ancient Monumentes as are yet extant'.

## — 1913 —

### HOUSES AND GARDENS BY E.L. LUTYENS
By Lawrence Weaver
Country Life; G Newnes: London, pp 344
1914 Reprinted with slight changes

1921 Abridged edition entitled *Lutyens Houses and Gardens* (see 1921)
1925 First edition reissued as *Houses and Gardens by Sir Edwin Lutyens, RA* (see 1925)
1981 First edition reissued by Antique Collectors' Club: Woodbridge
This book represents a record of Lutyens' work up to 1912, and helped to give the architect greater recognition. It contains 580 illustrations, which show Lutyens' genius in the design of the country house. Many chapters are based on articles from *Country Life*, including one on the restoration of Lindisfarne Castle, then the property of its editor, Edward Hudson. This book was the first of the *Country Life* folio series 'The Architects Library'.

*THE COUNTRY LIFE BOOK OF COTTAGES,*
*COSTING FROM £150 to £600*
By Lawrence Weaver
Country Life; G Newnes: London
C Scribner's Sons: New York, pp 231
1919 Second edition revised and enlarged
1926 Reissued as *Cottages: Their Planning, Design and Materials* (see 1926)
Richly illustrated with black and white photographs and plans, this book describes cottages designed by many leading architects of the day. Farm, town and holiday cottages are covered, with details of costs (a cottage in Essex by Mr Turner Powell cost £609 — 7¾d a cubic foot price, including drains and gas). The £600 cottages are of considerable size, some with laid-out gardens. Winning designs from *Country Life* competitions are included.

— 1914 —

*SMALL COUNTRY HOUSES:*
*THEIR REPAIR AND ENLARGEMENT*
Forty Examples Chosen From Five Centuries
Edited by Lawrence Weaver
Country Life; G Newnes: London
C Scribner's Sons: New York, pp 204

Dealing mainly with houses built before the 19th century, this book illustrates how they might be altered to meet the needs of the 20th while preserving their earlier character and fabric. The frontpiece shows five half-timbered cottages made into a single house. It is a companion volume to *Small Country Houses of Today* (volume 1, 1910; volume 2, 1919) and *The House and its Equipment* (1911). Together these three books represent a handsome record of the state of small country houses in England before the Great War.

## — 1915 —

### MEMORIALS AND MONUMENTS
Old and New: Two Hundred Subjects Chosen From Seven Centuries
By Lawrence Weaver
Country Life; G Newnes: London
C Scribner's Sons: New York, pp 479
This major work is well illustrated with photographs, plans and line drawings. The author lamented that 'today, many of the persons who are commonly called monumental masons bring to their task neither educated taste nor knowledge of good historical examples . . . In earlier days when monuments were not only honourable memorials of the dead, but works of art which gave joy to the living, the finest skills of architects and sculptors, working together, went to their making. The purpose of this book is not so much to provide a historical account of the development of those types of memorials which are the most suitable for present use, as to focus attention on good examples, old and new . . . This book is published in the hope that it may be useful to people who are considering memorials and that it may lead them to the artist rather than the trader'.

### THE STORY OF THE ROYAL SCOTS
By Lawrence Weaver
J Menzies: Edinburgh and Glasgow
C Scribner's Sons: New York, pp 272
As one of a proposed Country Life series of military histories,

this book was also published in an abridged version entitled *The Royal Scots: Five Centuries of Fighting* (pp 158). This unexpected work arose from Lawrence Weaver's 'long delight in reading Scottish history, and of much writing about the delightful fabric presented by the building of that history into the walls of Scottish castles'. The history of the regiment is recounted from the Battle of Agincourt to the Dardanelles campaign.

## — 1919 —

### SMALL COUNTRY HOUSES OF TODAY
Edited by Lawrence Weaver
Country Life; G Newnes: London
C Scribner's Sons: New York, pp 222
1922 Second edition revised
1925 Reissued as volume 2 of second series
As a second volume of descriptions of small country houses by contemporary British architects, this work followed the success of its 1910 predecessor (volume 1) and was reissued as volume 2 of a series which included a third volume by RR Phillips (1925).

### MANUAL FOR THE GUIDANCE OF COUNTY COUNCILS AND THEIR ARCHITECTS IN THE EQUIPMENT OF SMALL HOLDINGS
Edited by Lawrence Weaver
Board of Agriculture & Fisheries (HMSO): London, pp 53
This official publication arose from the author's experience as Director General of Land Settlement. Part I is on the planning and construction of cottages and part II is a discussion of farm buildings.

## — 1920 —

### VILLAGE CLUBS AND HALLS
By Lawrence Weaver
Country Life; G Newnes: London
C Scribner's Sons: New York, pp 112
Based on articles in *Country Life*, this book, illustrated with

black and white photographs and plans, describes village clubs and halls ranging from the one room hall at Harringworth to buildings of considerable size, some adapted from barns. The works of many of Lawrence Weaver's friends and contemporaries are featured.

### THE PLANNING AND PLANTING OF LITTLE GARDENS
By G Dillisone with a chapter by Lawrence Weaver
Country Life; G Newnes: London
C Scribner's Sons: New York, pp 134
The second chapter is by Weaver. The book contains the winning entries of a competition to design a garden for a small house. It includes illustrations of these with ideas for laying them out, and suggested flower arrangements.

# — 1921 —

### LUTYENS HOUSES AND GARDENS
By Sir Lawrence Weaver
Country Life; G Newnes: London
C Scribner's Sons: New York, pp 203
This is a smaller, abridged edition of *Houses and Gardens by E L Lutyens* (1913).

### REPORT OF PROCEEDINGS UNDER THE SMALL HOLDING COLONIES ACTS 1916 AND 1918
By Lawrence Weaver
Ministry of Agriculture and Fisheries (HMSO): London, pp 35
The Ministry owned or administered more than 13,000 acres of land on which ex-servicemen were settled and employed during the Great War. This report describes the organisation, agricultural use and building work on this farmland.

## — 1922 —

### REPORT OF PROCEEDINGS UNDER THE SMALL HOLDING COLONIES ACT 1916 AND 1918, AND SAILORS AND SOLDIERS (GIFTS FOR LAND SETTLEMENT ACT) 1916
By Lawrence Weaver
Ministry of Agriculture and Fisheries (HMSO): London, pp 63
This report follows that before and further describes the resettlement work directed by the author.

## — 1923 —

### THE EIGHTEENTH-CENTURY ARCHITECTURE OF BRISTOL
By CFW Dening
Preface by Sir Lawrence Weaver
Arrowsmith: Bristol, pp 191
Weaver's 'youthful hours of leisure were spent in eager study of mediaeval Bristol'. His preface was 'an act of penitence for his small love of eighteenth century landmarks' when young.

### SIR CHRISTOPHER WREN
### SCIENTIST, SCHOLAR AND ARCHITECT
By Sir Lawrence Weaver
Country Life; G Newnes: London
C Scribner's Sons: New York, pp 173
Published on the 200th anniversary of the death of Wren, this work was inspired by Weaver's acquisition of *Parentalia, or Memoirs of the Wrens* for the Royal Institute of British Architects. It contains attractive plates of many of Wren's London churches (by Edmund New) and photographs of portraits of the architect and his works.

## — 1924 —

### THE BOOK OF THE QUEEN'S DOLLS' HOUSE
Edited by AC Benson and Lawrence Weaver
Methuen: London, pp 249
An illustrated record of the Dolls' House, designed by

Lutyens, for Queen Mary. Ninety-two plates (24 in colour) offer views of most rooms and a large part of their contents. The book contains chapters on the architecture, by Lawrence Weaver, on the paintings by the Surveyor of the King's Pictures, on the textiles by the Keeper of Textiles of the Victoria & Albert Museum and on the kitchen of this most celebrated miniature house by Dymphna Ellis, holder of the Diploma and Teacher's Certificate of the National School of Cookery. It is a companion volume to *The Book Of The Queen's Dolls' House Library* by EV Lucas. Publication of both books, which were issued as a set, was limited to 1500 copies.

## EVERYBODY'S BOOK OF
## THE QUEEN'S DOLLS' HOUSE
By AC Benson and Lawrence Weaver
Daily Telegraph; Methuen: London, pp 160
This is an abbreviated version of the work before, condensed by F V Morley. Illustrated with both black and white and colour photographs, it records the incredible detail which went into Lutyens' playful creations: brushes and vacuum cleaners in the housemaids closet received attention equal to that of the five cars and lawn mower parked below. Everything was made to 1/12 scale, from despatch boxes to jam jars. This book was especially popular with children.

## — 1925 —

## HOUSES AND GARDENS BY SIR EDWIN LUTYENS, RA
By Sir Lawrence Weaver
Country Life; G Newnes: London
C Scribner's Sons: New York, pp 344
This is a third impression of the earlier work of 1913, unchanged apart from its title and enlarged size.

## EXHIBITIONS AND THE ARTS OF DISPLAY
By Sir Lawrence Weaver
Country Life; G Newnes: London, pp 106
The emphasis is on the quality of displays for advertising as a 'potential creator of public standards in good taste'. With 20

colour plates and many black and white illustrations this book is a major record of the British Empire Exhibition. Some photographs of halls of the Munich and Gothenburg exhibitions, which had influenced the author, are shown.

*ART IN INDUSTRY*
The Influence of Beauty in Commerce and Industry
By Sir Lawrence Weaver
British Commercial Gas Association: London, pp 12
This pamphlet records a speech delivered at the 13th annual conference of the British Commercial Gas Association, Liverpool in 1924.

— 1926 —

*COTTAGES:*
*THEIR PLANNING, DESIGN AND MATERIALS*
By Sir Lawrence Weaver
Country Life: London
C Scribner's Sons: New York, pp 402
The third edition of *The Country Life Book of Cottages* (1913) was revised and enlarged to include new ideas and methods generated by postwar demands for economical housing.

— 1927 —

*THE SCOTTISH NATIONAL WAR MEMORIAL*
At the Castle, Edinburgh; a Record of an Appreciation
By Sir Lawrence Weaver
Country Life: London, pp 42
1927 Four editions
1928 Fifth edition, revised
1929 Sixth edition
1931 Seventh edition
1933 Eighth edition
This guide to the memorial on the Rock at Edinburgh is reproduced from articles in *Country Life*. It includes 23 pages of black and white photographs of Lorimer's work. A version of

the guide, in which text and photographs are integrated, was also published.

# — 1928 —

## *TRADITION AND MODERNITY IN PLASTERWORK*
By Sir Lawrence Weaver
G Jackson and Sons: London, pp 63
Reprinted from *The Architectural Review,* this book in uniform with *High Wycombe Furniture* (1929), *Laminated Board and its Uses* (1930), *Gas Fires and their Settings* (1929) and *Tradition and Modernity in Metalwork* (1929) by the author. In characteristic fashion Lawrence Weaver illustrates the 'modern' use of plasterwork in interior design.

## *SOUVENIR BOOK OF THE QUEEN'S DOLLS' HOUSE*
Oxley and Son: Windsor, pp 74
This is a short guide, illustrated with black and white photographs, composed of abstracts from the larger earlier works of 1924.

## *THE PLACE OF ADVERTISING IN INDUSTRY*
By Sir Lawrence Weaver
The Advertising Association; Baynard Press: London, pp 30
Extracts reprinted from *The Quarterly Review,* 1928 as a slim book uniform with *The Function of a Service Advertising Agency, The Functions of Advertising and Salesmanship in Marketing, Does Advertising Benefit the Consumer?* and *Does Advertising Pay the Advertiser?* The pamphlet indicates Lawrence Weaver's growing concern with commercial affairs following his experience of the British Empire Exhibition.

## *DESIGN IN MODERN PRINTING:*
*THE YEAR BOOK OF THE DESIGN & INDUSTRIES*
*ASSOCIATION 1927-1928*
Edited by Joseph Thorp
Introduction by Sir Lawrence Weaver
E Benn: London, pp 159
Weaver introduced the first Year Book of the DIA dealing

specifically with one industry. Many of the illustrations depict typeface and layout suitable for advertisements. The Year Book of 1929-1930, entitled *The Face of the Land* (1930), was dedicated to the memory of 'Sir Lawrence Weaver, sometime president of the DIA and its steadfast friend.'

## — 1929 —

### *TRADITION AND MODERNITY IN METALWORK*
By Sir Lawrence Weaver
Birmingham Guild: Birmingham, pp 30
Reprinted from the *The Architectural Review,* 1928 and beautifully produced with plates of wrought iron gates, inn signs and door panels.

### *HIGH WYCOMBE FURNITURE*
By Sir Lawrence Weaver
Fanfare Press: London, pp 84
The first chapter is reprinted from *The Architectural Review,* 1929, with some additions and the second chapter from *The Architects' Journal,* 1929. It contains photographs of bodgers at work making chairs in the Buckinghamshire woods. High Wycombe was a centre of furniture making and 46 plates illustrate many pieces.

### *GAS FIRES AND THEIR SETTINGS*
By Sir Lawrence Weaver
Fanfare Press: London, pp 64
Expanded from an address to the British Commercial Gas Assoiation, York, 1928, published earlier as 'The Design of Gas Fires and their Settings' in *The Architectural Review.* The first gas fire designed to replace an existing coal grate is illustrated and the technical issues involved in the conversion of open to gas fires discussed.

### *ART IN INDUSTRY AND SALESMANSHIP,*
### *WITH SPECIAL REFERENCE TO THE WORK OF THE*
### *SILVERSMITH*
Curwen Press: London, pp 25
This slim work further illustrates the author's concern with the

relation between design and commerce. It is the record of a
lecture he delivered at Goldsmith's Hall in which he refers to
many of the exhibitions he visited abroad.

## — 1930 —

*LAMINATED BOARD AND ITS USES*
By Sir Lawrence Weaver
Fanfare Press: London, pp 82
A study of modern furniture decoration, edited by C Hussey,
reprinted from articles from *The Architectural Review, The
Architects' Journal* and *Shipping World*. It includes photographs
of pieces by Ernest Gimson.

Title page of Lawrence Weaver's first book.

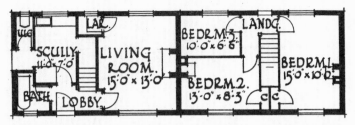

GROUND FLOOR. FIRST FLOOR.

*Lander and Kemp.*

443.—PAIR OF HIPPED ROOF COTTAGES IN HANDSIDE LANE.

*Lander and Kemp.*

444.—WELWYN : HIPPED ROOF PAIR IN HANDSIDE LANE.

and James. They adopted the gable and dormer as the characteristic features of their houses, but used the former in large simple units at the ends of the groups and provided good stretches of unbroken roof-line to connect the gabled ends. In each group a central through-passage was provided in the middle, to be seen in the plans, which show in each case three houses of the four. In both groups the presumption is that no maid is kept and there is a compactly arranged kitchen-dining-room (*see* plan, Fig. 438) and a large living-room. The planning of the middle two of the four is ingeniously devised in one of the

A typical page from *Cottages: Their Planning, Design and Materials*, 1926.

Nashdome House, Taplow, Buckinghamshire by Lutyens, 1909. Reproduced from *Houses and Gardens by E L Lutyens,* 1913.

Lawrence Weaver stands behind the mulberry tree planted by King George V at the opening of the National Institute of Agricultural Botany, Cambridge in 1921.

Exhibitions and the Arts of Display, 1925. Cover design by E McKnight
Kauffer.

# PART 2: ARTICLES

Articles are listed by year of publication, alphabetically by name of the periodical in which they appeared. This is followed by their volume and page numbers. Arabic numerals have been used throughout. Those articles published in *Country Life* are listed before those appearing in its weekly supplements. The latter are identified by their date of publication.

## — 1905 —

'English Lead Pipe-Heads I'.
*The Architectural Review* 18; 62–68

'English Lead Pipe-Heads II'.
*The Architectural Review* 18; 98–103

'English Lead Cisterns'.
*The Architectural Review* 18; 220–229

'English Lead Spout Heads'.
*Art Workers' Quarterly* 4; 156–162

'Some English Architectural Leadwork I'.
*The Burlington Magazine* 7; 270–280

'Some English Architectural Leadwork II'.
*The Burlington Magazine* 7; 428–434

'Some English Architectural Leadwork III'.
*The Burlington Magazine* 8; 103–109

'Earlshall, Fifeshire. The Seat of RW MacKenzie'.
*Country Life* 17; 942–950

'Lead Rain Waterheads'.
*Indoors & Out* 1; 243–246

'Lead Water Heads of the 16th & 17th Centuries'.
*Proceedings of the Society of Antiquaries of London* 20; 292–293

## — 1906 —

'Lead Garden Statuary'.
*American Homes & Gardens* 3; 2-4

'The Alleged Jervaulx Abbey Font'.
*The Architectural Review* 19; 87

'English Lead Fonts'.
*The Architectural Review* 19; 98-108

'Lead Garden Statues'.
*The Architectural Review* 20; 69-75

'Leadwork'. (lecture)
*The Builder* 40; 313-315

'Some English Architectural Leadwork IV. Lead Fonts'.
*The Burlington Magazine* 8; 246-256

'Some English Leadwork V. Garden Statues'.
*The Burlington Magazine* 8; 385-392

'Some English Leadwork VI. Portrait Statues'.
*The Burlington Magazine* 9; 97-106

'Some Architectural Leadwork VII. Scottish Lead Spires'.
*The Burlington Magazine* 9; 304-312

'London Leaded Steeples I'.
*The Burlington Magazine* 10; 82-88

'The Nurses' Home, Great Ormond Street'.
*Country Life* 19; 103-105

'Lead Pipeheads I'.
*Country Life* 20; 278-280

'Lead Pipeheads II'.
*Country Life* 20; 374-376

'Lead Pipeheads III'.
*Country Life* 20; 445-447

'Lead Cisterns'.
*Country Life* 20; 734-737

'Leadwork'.
*Journal of the Royal Institute of British Architects* 13; 257-260
(with FW Troup)

'Leadwork II The Earlier Lead Spires'.
*Journal of the Royal Institute of British Architects* 13; 260-275


**— 1907 —**

'A Note on Lead Coffins'.
*The Antiquary* 43; 372-374

'English Lead Spires'.
*The Architectural Review* 21; 2-14

'English Lead Fonts'.
*The Architectural Review* 21; 122

'Pipeheads in Oxford'.
*The Architectural Review* 22; 220

'Modern Leadwork I. Its Larger Use in Architecture'.
*The Architectural Review* 22; 221-229

'Modern Leadwork II. Rain-Water Heads'.
*The Architectural Review* 22; 268-273

'The Cass Statue'.
*The Architectural Review* 22; 333-334

'London Leaded Steeples II'.
*The Burlington Magazine* 10; 300-305

'London Leaded Steeples III'.
*The Burlington Magazine* 11; 88-96

'Lead Vases'.
*The Burlington Magazine* 12; 77-82

'Lead Garden Statues'.
*Country Life* 22; 7-10

'Forged Pilgrim's Tokens'.
*Country Life* 22; 216

'Lead Fonts'.
*Country Life* 22; 694-696

'Garden Statues of Lead'.
*Indoors & Out* 3; 202-204

## — 1908 —

'Modern Leadwork III. Cisterns, Fonts, Vases etc'.
*The Architectural Review* 23; 84-89

'Yorkshire Leadwork'.
*Country Life* 23; 82-85

'Lead Figures in Architecture'.
*Country Life* 23; 590-593

## — 1909 —

'Memorials to Wren'.
*The Architectural Review* 26; 175-183

'West Country Leadwork'. (letter)
*Country Life* 25; 144

'Imagination in Lead'.
*Country Life* 25; 548-549

'Of Garden Ornament'.
*Country Life* 25; 624-626

'Restoration Extraordinary'.
*Country Life* 26; 596-597

'Home Place, Holt. The Residence of the Reverend FM
Meyrich-Jones'.
*Country Life* 26; 634-642

'Some Furniture at Rothamstead'.
*Country Life* 25; (suppl June 19) 51-52

'Long Copse Ewhurst. Designed by Mr Alfred Powell'.
*Country Life;* (suppl Sept 11) 40-44

'Luckley, Wokingham. Designed by Mr Ernest Newton'.
*Country Life* 26; (suppl Sept 18) 40-44

'Architecture at the Hampstead Garden Suburb'.
*Country Life* 26; (suppl Sept 25) 42-48
26; (suppl Oct 2) 43-52

'External Leadwork'.
*Country Life* 26; (suppl Oct 2) 56-58

'A Cottage on Silchester Common. Designed by Mr Mervyn
E Macartney'.
*Country Life* 26; (suppl Oct 9) 46-50

'A Seaside Home in Thanet. Designed by Mr Arthur T Bolton'.
*Country Life* 26; (suppl Oct 16) 47-50

'The Barn, Whitley, Reading. Designed by Mr Frank
Chesterton'.
*Country Life* 26; (suppl Oct 23) 48-52

'Woodside, Graffham. Designed by Mr Hasley Ricardo'.
*Country Life* 26; (suppl Oct 30) 47-51

'Poyner's End, Near Hitchin. Designed by Mr Geoffrey
Lucas'.
*Country Life* 26; (suppl Nov 6) 49-51

'Bell Coombe, Saxlingham, Near Norwich. Designed by
Mr FW Troup'.
*Country Life* 26; (suppl Nov 13) 49-53

'Breach House, Cholsey. Designed by Mr Edward P Warren'.
*Country Life* 26; (suppl Nov 20) 43-52

'Angrove House, Crowborough. Designed by Mr Fairfax
B Wade'.
*Country Life* 26; (suppl Nov 27) 45-46

'The English House'.
*Country Life* 26; (suppl Dec 4) 106-122

'Beaumonts, Edenbridge, Kent. Designed by Mr Robert Weir
Schultz'.
*Country Life* 26; (suppl Dec 25) 32-36

'Leadwork at Haddon Hall'.
*Country & Town* 1; 53-54

'Plumbing as an Art'.
*Plumbing Trade Journal* 2; No 13, 20-22
2; No 14; 20-24

'The Interleaved Copy of Wren's Parentalia'.
*Proceedings of the Society of Antiquaries of London* 22; 1-7

'The Interleaved Copy of Wren's Parentalia with Manuscript Insertions'.
*Proceedings of the Society of Antiquaries of London* 22; 524-530

# — 1910 —

'The Art of the Leadworker'. (lecture)
*The Builder* 48; 228-229

'Some Letters of Sir Christopher Wren'.
*Country Life* 27; 41-44

'Moundsmere Manor, Basingstoke. The Seat of Mr Wilfred Buckley'.
*Country Life* 27; 378-385

'New Place, Shedfield, Hampshire. The Seat of Mr Arden Franklyn'.
*Country Life* 27; 522-531

'Standen, East Grinstead. A Residence of Mr James S Beale'.
*Country Life* 27; 666-672

'The First French Book on Architecture'.
*Country Life* 27; 807-809

'Avon Tyrrell, Christchurch, Hampshire. A Seat of Lord Manners'.
*Country Life* 27; 846-852

'Heathcote, Ilkley, Yorkshire. The Residence of Mr J T Hemingway'.
*Country Life* 28; 54-65

'Sandhouse, Witley, Surrey. The Residence of Mr Joseph King'.
*Country Life* 28; 296-302

'Shaw House, Newbury. The Seat of the Hon Mrs Farquar'.
*Country Life* 28; 328-338

'Hinton Admiral, Hampshire. A Seat of Sir George Meyrick Bart'.
*Country Life* 28; 494-498

'Lympne Castle, Kent. The Seat of Mr F J Tennant'.
*Country Life* 28; 682-689

'Nether Swell Manor, Stow-on-the-Wold. The Residence of Mr Walter Montagu Scott'.
*Country Life* 28; 754-760

'Wych Cross Place, Forest Row, Sussex. The Residence of Mr Douglas W Freshfield'.
*Country Life* 28; 934-940

'Three Little Houses. Designed by Mr P Morley Horder'.
*Country Life* 27; (suppl Jan 1) 35-39

'Inverleith Manor, Norwich. Designed by Mr P Morley Horder and Mr A G Wyand'.
*Country Life* 27; (suppl Jan 8) 37-41

'Acremead, Crockham Hill, Kent. Designed by Mr Cecil Brewer'.
*Country Life* 27; (suppl Feb 5) 37-41

'Rosewall, Wimbledon. Designed by Mr M H Baillie Scott'.
*Country Life* 27; (suppl Feb 19) 41-45

'Poynetts, Chilworth, Surrey'.
*Country Life* 27; (suppl Mar 5) 43-47

'How Green, Hever, Kent'.
*Country Life* 27; (suppl Mar 12) 47-51

'The Cobbles, Walton Heath. Designed by Mr L Stanley Crosbie'.
*Country Life* 27; (suppl Apr 2) 43-44

'The Hurst, Moseley, Birmingham. Designed by Mr W H
Bidlake'.
*Country Life* 27; (suppl Apr 9) 51-59

'The Chimney Corner, Walton Heath, Surrey. Designed by
Mr Guy Dawber'.
*Country Life* 27; (suppl Apr 16) 51-52

'The Pasture House, Luffenham, Rutland. Designed by Mr C
F A Voysey'.
*Country Life* 27; (suppl Apr 23) 49-52

'The Hurst, Four Oaks, Sutton Coldfield. Designed by
Professor W R Lethaby'.
*Country Life* 27; (suppl May 7) 53-58

'Gilham's Birch, Rotherfield, Sussex. Designed by Mr E J
May'.
*Country Life* 27; (suppl May 14) 53-58

'Littlewick Meadow, Horsell, Surrey. Designed by
Mr Maurice Pocock'.
*Country Life* 27; (suppl May 21) 51-53

'West Chart, Limpsfield, Surrey. Designed by Mr E Turner
Powell'.
*Country Life* 27; (suppl May 28) 55-59

'Elm Tree Cottage, Farnham, Surrey. Designed by Mr Harold
Falkner'.
*Country Life* 27; (suppl June 4) 57-58

'The Red House, Upton, Kent. Designed by Mr Philip Webb'.
*Country Life* 27; (suppl June 11) 51-55

'South Hill, Hook Heath, Woking. Designed by Mr Horace
Field'.
*Country Life* 27; (suppl June 25) 7-11

'Redlands, Four Oaks, Sutton Coldfield. Designed by Mr
Charles E Bateman'.
*Country Life* 28; (suppl July 9) 7-11

'Bishopsbarn, Yorks. Designed by Mr Walter H Brierley'.
*Country Life* 28; (suppl July 16) 7-11

'New Place, Welwyn, Herts. Designed by Mr Philip Webb'.
*Country Life* 28; (suppl July 23) 7-8

'A Thatched House in Suffolk, with Additions by Mr Charles Spooner'.
*Country Life* 28; (suppl July 30) 7-10

'Sandyhurst, Northwood. Designed by Mr H G Coales and Mr H W Johnson'.
*Country Life* 28; (suppl Aug 6) 7-8

'Madeley, Stevenage, Herts. Designed by Mr H P G Maule'.
*Country Life* 28; (suppl Aug 13) 7-8

'Little Frankley, Hook Heath, Woking. Designed by Mr Horace Field'.
*Country Life* 28; (suppl Aug 20) 7-8

'Brookside, Brampton, Chesterfield. Designed by Mr Percy B Houfton'.
*Country Life* 28; (suppl Aug 27) 7-11

'A Brick House, near Farnham. Designed by Mr Harold Falkner'.
*Country Life* 28; (suppl Sep 3) 7-10

'Highlands, Woldingham, Surrey. Designed by Mr H C Trimnell'.
*Country Life* 28; (suppl Sep 10) 7-11

'Seal Hollow, Sevenoaks. Designed by Mr H Baillie Scott'.
*Country Life* 28; (suppl Sep 17) 7-11

'Middlefield, Great Shelford, near Cambridge. Designed by Mr E L Lutyens'.
*Country Life* 28; (suppl Sep 24) 7-11

'The Homestead, Frinton-on-Sea. Designed by Mr C F A Voysey'.
*Country Life* 28; (suppl Oct 1) 7-11

'The Old Pond House, Wimbledon. Designed by Mr Albert Moore'.
*Country Life* 28; (suppl Oct 8) 7-11

'Whixley Hall, near York and its Reparation by Mr Walter Brierley'.
*Country Life* 28; (suppl Oct 15) 7-11

'Coldicote, Moreton-in-the-Marsh. Designed by Mr Guy Dawber'.
*Country Life* 28; (suppl Oct 22) 7-11

'Bengeo House, Hertford. Designed by Mr Walter Cave'.
*Country Life* 28; (suppl Oct 29) 7-11

'Sunnymede, Wadhurst. Designed by Mr Frank Chesterton'.
*Country Life* 28; (suppl Nov 5) 7-8

'Upmeads, Stafford. Designed by Mr Edgar Wood'.
*Country Life* 28; (suppl Nov 12) 7-11

'Guiseley Rectory, near Leeds and its Reparation by Sir Charles Nicholson and Mr H C Corlette'.
*Country Life* 28; (suppl Nov 19) 7-11

'The Home of the New President of the R.I.B.A. (Mr Leonard Stokes)'.
*Country Life* 28; (suppl Dec 3) 30-34

'Caldecott, Caldy. Designed by Mr Hastwell Grayson'.
*Country Life* 28; (suppl Dec 10) 7-8

'Croswell Cottages, Mayford, Woking. Designed by Mr Horace Field'.
*Country Life* 28; (suppl Dec 17) 8-12

'Hambleton Hall, Rutland'.
*Country Life* 28; (suppl Dec 24) 7-10

'Copyhold, Chobham, Surrey, and its Enlargement by Mr Theophilus Allen'.
*Country Life* 28; (suppl Dec 31) 7-11

'The Art and History of British Leadwork'. (lectures)
*Journal of the Royal Society of Arts* 58; 1054-1061
58; 1076-1083

# — 1911 —

'Wren's "Parentalia"'.
*Architects' and Builders' Journal* 33; 668-673

'Ardenrun Place, Blindley Heath, Surrey. The Residence of Mr H H Konig'.
*Country Life* 29; 90-96

'Dawpool, Thurstaston. The Residence of Sir Herbert Roberts Bart MP'.
*Country Life* 29; 234-240

'Temple Dinsley, Herts. The Residence of Mr H G Fenwick'.
*Country Life* 29; 562-572

'Ardkinglas, Argyllshire. A Seat of Sir Andrew Noble Bt KCB'.
*Country Life* 29; 746-754

'West Stow Hall, Suffolk. The Property of the Earl of Cadogan'.
*Country Life* 29; 848-851

'Holyrood Palace II.
The Scottish Palace of His Majesty George V'.
*Country Life* 30; 132-138

'Normanby Park, Burton-on-Stather, Lincolnshire. The Seat of Sir Berkeley Sheffield Bart'.
*Country Life* 30; 170-176

'Pinkie House, Musselburgh. The Seat of Sir Alexander Hope Bart'.
*Country Life* 30; 240-246

'Caroline Park, Midlothian. A Seat of the Duke of Buccleuch KGKT'.
*Country Life* 30; 276-284

'Grey Walls. Gullane. A Residence of Mr William James'.
*Country Life* 30; 374-380

'Hatton House, Midlothian. The Seat of Mr James McKelvie'.
*Country Life* 30; 408-414

'Dalkeith Place, Near Edinburgh. A Seat of the Duke of Buccleuch KG.'.
*Country Life* 30; 510-519

'Dolobarn, Chislehurst. Designed by Mr Curtis Green'.
*Country Life* 29; (suppl Jan 7) 7-10

'Kennet Orley, Woolhampton. Berkshire. Designed by Mr Mervyn Macartney'.
*Country Life* 29; (suppl Jan 14) 7-10

'Icknield Cottage, Wendover. Designed by Mr Maurice Pocock'.
*Country Life* 29; (suppl Jan 21) 7-11

'The Vineyards, Great Baddow, Essex, and its Reparation by Mr Arnold Mitchell'.
*Country Life* 29; (suppl Jan 28) 7-11

'Chussex, Walton-on-the-Hill. Designed by Mr E L Lutyens'.
*Country Life* 29; (suppl Feb 4) 7-11

'Moorcraft, Moor Green, Birmingham. Designed by Mr Herbert T Buckland and Mr Ernest R Bewley'.
*Country Life* 29; (suppl Feb 11) 7-11

'Four Little Houses at Llanfairfechan. Designed by Mr Herbert C North'.
*Country Life* 29; (suppl Feb 18) 7-11

'Morton House, Hatfield, and its Reparation by Mr A Winter Rose'.
*Country Life* 29; (suppl Feb 25) 7-11

'Hen Grove, St. Leonards, Bucks. Designed by Mr P Morley Horder'.
*Country Life* 29; (suppl Mar 11) 7-11

'High Coxlease, Lyndhurst, Hants. Designed by Professor W R Lethaby'.
*Country Life* 29; (suppl Mar 11) 7-11

'Woolston Grange, near Taunton, and its Alteration by Mr Horace Farquarson'.
*Country Life* 29; (suppl Mar 18) 7-8

'A South Country House. Designed by Mr Philip Webb'.
*Country Life* 29; (suppl Mar 25) 7-11

'Lesser Country houses of the 16th Century.
Priory Place, Blythburgh, Suffolk'.
*Country Life* 29; (suppl Apr 1) 7-11

'Lodge Style, Combe Down, Bath. Designed by Mr C F A
Voysey'.
*Country Life* 29; (suppl Apr 8) 7-11

'Some Cottages. Designed by Mr A L Clough'.
*Country Life* 29; (suppl Apr 15) 7-11

'Castle Bromwich Rectory, Warwickshire. Designed by
Mr Charles Bateman'.
*Country Life* 29; (suppl Apr 22) 7-11

'St. Peter's Vicarage, Ealing. Designed by Mr P Morley Horder'.
*Country Life* 29; (suppl Apr 29) 7-11

'The Problem of the Cheap Cottage'.
*Country Life* 29; (Architectural suppl Apr 29) 16-22

'Lamarsh Rectory. Designed by Mr R M F Huddart'.
*Country Life* 29; (suppl May 6) 7-11

'St. Anne's Vicarage, Duddeston, Birmingham, as Altered by
Mr W H Bidlake'.
*Country Life* 29; (suppl May 13) 7-11

'Stonywell Cottage, Charnwood Forest. Designed by
Mr Ernest W Gimson and Built by Mr Detmar Blow'.
*Country Life* 29; (suppl May 20) 7-11

'A Yeoman's House of the 16th Century. Quennell House,
Plaistow, Sussex, and its Repair by Mr Basil Stallybrass'.
*Country Life* 29; (suppl May 27) 8-12

'The Exhibition of Houses at Gidea Park, Romford'.
*Country Life* 29; (suppl June 3) 13-20
29; (suppl June 10) 7-10

'Hedgeblooms, Welwyn, Herts. Designed by Mr H V Ashley
and Mr Winton Newman'.
*Country Life* 29; (suppl June 17) 7-11

'Woodgate, Four Oaks. Designed by Mr W H Bidlake'.
*Country Life* 29; (suppl June 24) 7–11

'Winterbourne, Birmingham. Designed by Mr C L Ball'.
*Country Life* 29; (suppl July 1) 7–8

'Crathorne, Weybridge. Designed by Mr Vivien Jackson'.
*Country Life* 30; (suppl July 8) 7–11

'Littleholme, Guildford. Designed by Mr C F A Voysey'.
*Country Life* 30; (suppl July 15) 7–11

'Folly Farm, Sulhampstead, Berkshire. Designed by Mr E L
Lutyens'.
*Country Life* 30; (suppl July 22) 7–11

'Pardlestone Cottage, Kilve, Somerset. Designed by
Mr Charles Spooner'.
*Country Life* 30; (suppl July 29) 7–8

'Wayside, Rothley, Leicestershire. Designed by Mr T
Millwood Wilson'.
*Country Life* 30; (suppl Aug 5) 7–8

'Mellbreak, Byfleet, Surrey. Designed by Mr Basil Procter'.
*Country Life* 30; (suppl Aug 12) 7–8

'Yewlands, Hoddeston, Herts. Designed by Mr Geoffrey
Lucas'.
*Country Life* 30; (suppl Aug 19) 7–8

'A Gardener's Cottage at Goldings, Hertford. Designed by
Mr H S Goodhart-Rendel'.
*Country Life* 30; (suppl Aug 26) 7–8

'Fairshot Court, Sandridge, Herts. Designed by Mr A F
Royds'.
*Country Life* 30; (suppl Sep 2) 7–10

'Wool Manor House, Dorset. Sketched by Mr Harold Falkner'.
*Country Life* 30; (suppl Sep 9) 7–11

'The Murrel, Aberdour, Fife. Designed by Mr F W Deas'.
*Country Life* 30; (suppl Sep 16) 7–11

'Lea Cottage, Charnwood Forest, Leicestershire. Designed by Mr Ernest Gimson and Built by Mr Detmar Blow'.
*Country Life* 30; (suppl Sep 23) 7-10

'Yockley House, Camberley, Surrey. Designed by Professor Reginald Blomfield ARA'.
*Country Life* 30; (suppl Sep 30) 7-10

'King John's Farm, Chorley Wood, Herts, and its Repair and Enlargement'.
*Country Life* 30; (suppl Oct 7) 7-12

'Cheyne Cottage, Stanmore, Middlesex. Designed by Mr James B Scott'.
*Country Life* 30; (suppl Oct 14) 7-8

'Dawstone, Windermere. Designed by the Late Mr Dan Gibson'.
*Country Life* 30; (suppl Oct 21) 7-11

'New Garden Terrace, Foxbury, Chislehurst. Designed by Mr Maurice E Webb'.
*Country Life* 30; (suppl Oct 28) 7-8

'Laverockdale, near Edinburgh. Designed by Sir Robert Lorimer'.
*Country Life* 30; (suppl Nov 4) 7-12

'Monkton House, Chilgrove, Sussex. Designed by Mr E L Lutyens'.
*Country Life* 30; (suppl Nov 11) 7-12

'Marrowells, Walton-on-Thames. Designed by Mr A Winter Rose'.
*Country Life* 30; (suppl Nov 18) 7-12

'Town Planning Notes.
Architecture at the Hampstead Garden Suburb'.
*Country Life* 30; (suppl Dec 2) 26-36

'Dene Place, West Horsley, Surrey'.
*Country Life* 30; (suppl Dec 9) 7-8

'The New Home of the British School at Rome'.
*Country Life* 30; (suppl Dec 16) 7-11

'The Burlington-Devonshire Collection of Drawings with Special Reference to the Relation between Inigo Jones and John Webb'. (Discussion of a paper by JA Gotch)
*Journal of the Royal Institute of British Architects* 18; 337-338

'The Interleaved Copy of Wren's Parentalia with Manuscript Insertions'.
*Journal of Royal Institute of British Architects* 18; 569-585
This article records the acquisition of Wren's Parentalia by Lawrence Weaver and its presentation by him to the RIBA on June 26th 1911.

'British Leadwork. Its Art and History'. (lecture)
*Plumbing Trade Journal* 3; No 35, 28-31

'The Art and History of British Leadwork'. (lecture)
*Plumbing Trade Journal* 3; No 37, 26-28

## — 1912 —

'Some Scottish Houses of the Rennaissance'. (lecture)
*The Builder* 52; 448-449

'Moor Park, Hertfordshire. The Seat of Lord Ebury'.
*Country Life* 31; (suppl 31) 18-26
31; 56-62

'Westbrook, Godalming. The Residence of Mr Thackeray Turner'.
*Country Life* 31; 92-96

'Falkland Palace, Fife. The Property of Lord Ninian Crichton Stuart MP'.
*Country Life* 31; 130-139

'The Court House, Somersetshire. The Seat of Mr Alexander Wittrell'.
*Country Life* 31; 168-175

'Chesters, Northumberland. The Seat of Mrs N G Clayton'.
*Country Life* 31; 244-248

'Balcaskie, Fife. The Seat of Sir Ralph Anstruther Bart'.
*Country Life* 31, 318-326

'Claydon House, Buckinghamshire. The Seat of Sir Harry
Verney Bart MP'.
*Country Life* 31; 356–364
31; 394–402

'Ewelme Down, Oxon. The Residence of Mr Frank Lawson'.
*Country Life* 31; 430–436

'Balls Park, Hertford. The Seat of Sir George Faudel-Phillips
Bart'.
*Country Life* 31; 578–587

'Wren's House and Pallant House, Chichester'.
*Country Life* 31; 614–619

'Lambay, Ireland. The Seat of the Hon Cecil Baring'.
*Country Life* 31; 650–658

'Bronze Garden Vases'.
*Country Life* 31; 976–977

'Kinross House, Kinross, the Seat of Sir Basil Montgomery
Bart'.
*Country Life* 32; 54–60
32; 90–95

'Old Place of Mochrum, Galloway, the Seat of the Marquess
of Bute'.
*Country Life* 32; 162–167

'Castle Bromwich Hall, Warwickshire, the Seat of Viscount
Newport'.
*Country Life* 32; 228–235

'Winton Castle, East Lothian. A Seat of Mrs Nisbet Hamilton
Ogilvy of Belhaven, Dilveston and Winton'.
*Country Life* 32; 260–267

'Nashdom, Taplow, the Residence of HH Princess Alexis
Dolgorouki'.
*Country Life* 32; 292–298

'Fyvie Castle, Aberdeenshire. The Seat of Lord Leith of Fyvie'.
*Country Life* 32; 388–392

'Three Houses near Cape Town'.
*Country Life* 32; 420-426

'Bovey House, Beer, Devon. The Residence of Mr A Locke Radford'.
*Country Life* 32; 674-679

'Midmar Castle and Barra Castle, Aberdeenshire'.
*Country Life* 32; 710-715

'Cliveden, Bucks. The Seat of Mr Waldorf Astor'.
*Country Life* 32; 808-818
32; 854-859

'The Walled Garden at Edzell Castle'.
*Country Life* 32; 859-862

'Hill of Tarvit, Fife. The Seat of Mr FB Sharp'.
*Country Life* 32; 926-930

'Village Halls and Clubs'.
*Country Life* 31; (suppl Jan 6) 7-8

'Saxby's, Chislehurst and its Remodelling by Mr E J May'.
*Country Life* 31; (suppl Jan 13) 7-8

'Oak and Plaster Cottages in Oxfordshire. Designed by Mr Maxwell Ayrton'.
*Country Life* 31; (suppl Jan 20) 7-8

'Lingy Acre, Portinscale, Keswick. Designed by M W H Ward'.
*Country Life* 31; (suppl Jan 27) 7-11

'Cray, Shiplake. Designed by Mr Maberly-Smith'.
*Country Life* 31; (suppl Feb 3) 7-8

'Dyke Nook, Accrington. Designed by Mr Walter Brierley'.
*Country Life* 31; (suppl Feb 10) 7-11

'The Old Court House. The Property of the National Trust'.
*Country Life* 31; (suppl Feb 17) 7-8

'Longmeadow, Bovingdon. Designed by Mr Walter E Hewitt'.
*Country Life* 31; (suppl Feb 24) 7-8

'Country Buildings of Today: Six Village Halls'.
*Country Life* 31; (suppl Mar 2) 7–12

'An Old Cottage at Peaslake, Surrey'.
*Country Life* 31; (suppl Mar 9) 7–8

'Keldwith, Windermere. Designed by Mr H L North'.
*Country Life* 31; (suppl Mar 23) 7–11

'Four Cottages of Varying Type'.
*Country Life* 31; (suppl Mar 30) 7–11

'The Court House, Broadway and its Remodelling by Mr E Guy Dawber'.
*Country Life* 31; (suppl Apr 6) 7–11

'Birkett House, Winster, Lancashire. Designed by Mr Dan Gibbon'.
*Country Life* 31; (suppl Apr 13) 7–11

'Combelands, Pulborough, Sussex, and its Remodelling by Mr Edward Prior'.
*Country Life* 31; (suppl Apr 20) 7–11

'The Pleasance, Gullane. Designed by Mr Sydney Mitchell'.
*Country Life* 31; (suppl Apr 27) 7–11

'Country Buildings of Today: Some Dog Kennels'.
*Country Life* 31; (suppl May 4) 7–11

'Country Buildings of Today: Four Golf Club Houses'.
*Country Life* 31; (suppl May 11) 7–11

'Architecture at the Royal Academy'.
*Country Life* 31; (suppl May 25) 29–34

'Plewland, Haslemere. Designed by Mr Falconer Macdonald'.
*Country Life* 31; (suppl June 1) 7–8

'A Lesser Country House of the 16th Century.
East Mascals, Lindfield, Sussex'.
*Country Life* 31; (suppl June 8) 7–8

'Perrot Cottage, Graffham, Sussex. Designed by Mr Leonard Williams'.
*Country Life* 31; (suppl June 15) 7–8

'A House in an Oxfordshire Wood and its Alteration by
Mr Maxwell Ayrton'.
*Country Life* 31; (suppl June 22) 7-11

'A Lesser Country House of the 16th Century.
Vann, Hambleton, Surrey, and its Alteration by Mr W D
Caroe'.
*Country Life* 31; (suppl June 29) 7-11

'A Lesser Country House of the 16th Century.
Pittencrieff, Dunfermline and its Remodelling by Sir Robert
Lorimer'.
*Country Life* 32; (suppl July 6) 7-8

'A Lesser Country House of the 16th Century.
Little Boarhunt, Liphook, Hants and its Remodelling by
Mr H Inigo Triggs'.
*Country Life* 32; (suppl July 13) 7-11

'Hurtwood Edge, Ewhurst, Surrey. Designed by Mr Arthur
Bolton'.
*Country Life* 32; (suppl July 20) 7-11

'Some Cottages for Smallholdings'.
*Country Life* 32; (suppl July 27) 7-11

'Little Ellers, Portinscale'.
*Country Life* 32; (suppl Aug 3) 7-8

'Englefield, Bickley Park, Kent'.
*Country Life* 32; (suppl Aug 10) 7-11

'Cragwood, Windermere. Designed by Mr Frank B Dunkerley'.
*Country Life* 32; (suppl Aug 17) 7-11

'Little Langleys, Petersfield. Designed by Mr Horace
Farquarson'.
*Country Life* 32; (suppl Aug 24) 7-8

'Rockyfield, Ulverscroft, Leicestershire'.
*Country Life* 32; (suppl Aug 31) 7-8

'Broad Dene, Haslemere. Designed by Mr W F Unsworth and
Mr Inigo Triggs'.
*Country Life* 32; (suppl Sep 7) 7-11

'A Lesser Country House of the 16th Century.
The Grove, Mill Hill and its Remodelling by Mr Stanley
Hamp'.
*Country Life* 32; (suppl Sep 14) 7–11

'The Old End, Forest Row, Sussex. Designed by Mr E Turner
Powell'.
*Country Life* 32; (suppl Sep 21) 7–8

'Kestrel Grove, Bushey Heath and its Remodelling by
Mr Harold Goslett'.
*Country Life* 32; (suppl Oct 5) 7–8

'Redholm, Walton Heath, Surrey. Designed by Mr P Morley
Horder'.
*Country Life* 32; (suppl Oct 19) 7–11

'Fellside, Bowness. Designed by the Late Mr Dan Gibson'.
*Country Life* 32; (suppl Oct 26) 7–8

'The Dormy House, Walton Heath. Designed by Mr E L
Lutyens'.
*Country Life* 32; (suppl Nov 9) 7–11

'The Mound, Long Crendon and its Enlargement by Mr S
Austin Gomme'.
*Country Life* 32; (suppl Nov 16) 7–11

'Kemsing Village Hall. Designed by Mr Godfrey Pinkerton'.
*Country Life* 32; (suppl Nov 23) 7–11

'The Small House, Lavant, Sussex. Designed by Professor
E S Prior'.
*Country Life* 32; (suppl Nov 30) 7–8

'Two South African Houses. Designed by the Late Frances
Masey'.
*Country Life* 32; (suppl Dec 7) 15–16

'Little Pednor Farm and its Enlargement by Mr Edwin
Forbes'.
*Country Life* 32; (suppl Dec 14) 7–11

'Some Houses at Letchworth. Designed by Mr Barry Parker'.
*Country Life* 32; (suppl Dec 21) 7–11

'Beechlaw, Puttenham. Designed by Mr H P G Maule'.
*Country Life* 32; (suppl Dec 28) 7-8

## — 1913 —

'The Birmingham Architectural Association: Leadwork'.
*The Builder* 105; 697

'Great Dixter, Sussex. The Residence of Mr Nathaniel Lloyd'.
*Country Life* 33; 18-26

'Marlow Place, Great Marlow. The Residence of Mr W Niven'.
*Country Life* 33; 54-58

'Cadhay, Devon. The Residence of Mr W C D Whellan'.
*Country Life* 33; 90-97

'Pollok House, Renfrewshire. The Seat of Sir John Stirling-Maxwell Bart'.
*Country Life* 33; 126-133

'Careston Castle, Forfarshire. The Seat of Mr W Shaw Adamson'.
*Country Life* 33; 310-314

'Drumlanrig Castle, Dumfrieshire. The Seat of the Duke of Buccleuch & Queensbury'.
*Country Life* 33; 382-390

'Marsh Court, Hampshire. The Residence of Mr Herbert Johnson'.
*Country Life* 33; 562-571

'Crathes Castle, Aberdeenshire. The Seat of Sir Thomas Burnett Bart'.
*Country Life* 33; 598-603

'Small Holders' Cottages'.
*Country Life* 33; 610-611

'Rowallan, Ayrshire. The Seat of Lord Rowallan'.
*Country Life* 34; 420-425

'The Search for Cheapness'.
*Country Life* 34; 556-557
34; 615-616

'Lullingstone Castle, Kent. The Seat of Rt Hon Sir William Hart Dyke Bart'.
*Country Life* 34; 602-608

'Three Houses at Farnham. Designed by Mr Harold Falkner'.
*Country Life* 33; (suppl Jan 4) 8-12

'The Hillside Garden at Owlpen Manor'.
*Country Life* 33; (suppl Jan 11) 7-11

'High Moss, Portinscale, Keswick'.
*Country Life* 33; (suppl Jan 18) 7-8

'Some Types of Cottage'.
*Country Life* 33; (suppl Jan 25) 7-11

'A Lesser Country House of the 16th Century. Nethergate House, Clare, Suffolk and its Repair by Mr H Munro-Cautley'.
*Country Life* 33; (suppl Feb 1) 7-12

'Hillside, Gledhow, Leeds and its Enlargement by Mr Sydney Kitson'.
*Country Life* 33; (suppl Feb 8) 7-11

'Bidsworth House, Broadway. Designed by Mr Guy Dawber'.
*Country Life* 33; (suppl Feb 15) 7-11

'Shorne Hill, Totton, Hants. Designed by Mr Ernest Wilmott'.
*Country Life* 33; (suppl Feb 22) 11-15

'Gerston, Storrington, Sussex. Designed by Mr Turner Powell'.
*Country Life* 33; (suppl Mar 1) 7-12

'Ravensbury Manor, Mitcham. Designed by Mr Horatio Porter and Mr Percy Newton'.
*Country Life* 33; (suppl Mar 8) 7-11

'Hascombe Court, Near Godalming. Designed by Mr John Coleridge'.
*Country Life* 33; (suppl Apr 5) 8-11

'Models of Small Country Houses of Today'.
*Country Life* 33; (suppl Apr 19) 7-11

'White Craggs, Ambleside. Designed by Mr Dan Gibson'.
*Country Life* 33; (suppl Apr 26) 7–11

'A House at El Assassif in the Egyptian Desert. Designed by Mr Palmer Jones'.
*Country Life* 33; (suppl May 3) 7–11

'The Hoo, Willingdon, Sussex and its Enlargement by Mr E L Lutyens'.
*Country Life* 33; (suppl May 10) 7–11

'Hovenden House, Fleet, Lincolnshire. Designed by Mr J E Dixon–Spain'.
*Country Life* 33; (suppl May 24) 7–8

'Walden, Croydon. Designed by Mr Curtis Green'.
*Country Life* 33; (suppl May 31) 7–8

'At the Royal Academy of Architecture'.
*Country Life* 33; (suppl June 7) 19–28

'The Country Life Architects Competition for Designs of a House to be Built in Sussex.
Notes on the Designs by the Judges E L Lutyens, P Morley Horder, L Weaver'.
*Country Life* 33; (suppl June 28) 7–30

'A Lesser Country House of the 16th Century.
Old Castle, Dallington, Sussex and its Enlargement by Mr Ernest Newton'.
*Country Life* 34; (suppl July 5) 8–11

'A Lesser Country House of the 16th Century.
Paycocke's, Coggeshall, Essex'.
*Country Life* 34; (suppl July 12) 7–11

'A Lesser Country House of the 16th Century.
Ruckmans, Oakwood Hill, Surrey and its Enlargement by Mr E L Lutyens'.
*Country Life* 34; (suppl July 19) 7–11

'Aswardby Hall, Spilsby, Lincolnshire. Designed by Mr H M Fletcher'.
*Country Life* 34; (suppl July 26) 8–11

'A Cottage of the 16th Century. Little Lodge, Chailey, Sussex and its Enlargement by Mr Walter Godfrey'.
*Country Life* 34; (suppl Aug 2) 7-11

'Hydon Ridge, Hambledon, Surrey'.
*Country Life* 34; (suppl Aug 9) 7-8

'Willinghurst, Cranleigh, Sussex. Designed by Mr Philip Webb'.
*Country Life* 34; (suppl Aug 23) 7-8

'Two Houses at Stanstead, Essex. Designed by Mr John S Lee'.
*Country Life* 34; (suppl Aug 30) 8-11

'Greyfriars, Tilford, Surrey'.
*Country Life* 34; (suppl Sept 6) 8-12

'A Lesser Country House of the 16th Century.
Rake House, Milford, Surrey'.
*Country Life* 34; (suppl Sept 13) 7-11

'The West Surrey Golf Club House, Milford. Designed by Mr Arthur A Messer'.
*Country Life* 34; (suppl Sept 20) 7-11

'Modern Scottish Architecture. The Work of Sir Robert Lorimer'.
*Country Life* 34; (Architectural suppl Sept 27) 17-51
Dunderave Castle 19-22
Barton Hartshorne Manor, Bucks 22-23
Formakin, Renfrewshire 24-28
The New Library, St Andrews University 28-29
The Ceiling at Ardkinglas 29-31
Brackenbrough, Cumberland 31
Town Planning at Galashiels 31-32
Reconstructions after Fire and New Interiors 32-39
St Peter's Church, Edinburgh 39-40
Some Smaller Houses 40-47
Rhu-Na-Haven 47
The Queen's Chair at St Giles Cathedral etc 48-51

'A Town House of the 16th Century. Crosby Hall and its Rebuilding, under the care of Mr Walter Godfrey'.
*Country Life* 34; (suppl Oct 4) 8-15

'Two Lesser Country Houses of the 16th Century.
The Priests House and the Manor house, West Hoathley,
Sussex and their Repair by Mr maurice Pocock'.
*Country Life* 34; (suppl Oct 11) 7-11

'Rest Harrow, Sandwich. Designed by Mr Paul Phipps'.
*Country Life* 34; (suppl Oct 18) 8-12

'The Wharf, Sutton Courtenay, Berkshire. Designed by Mr
Walter Cave'.
*Country Life* 34; (suppl Oct 25) 7-11

'Foldsdown, Thursley, Surrey. Designed by Mr Davidson'.
*Country Life* 34; (suppl Nov 1) 7-11

'A Country House of the English Regency.
Lyne Grove and its Enlargement by Mr Arthur T Bolton'.
*Country Life* 34; (suppl Nov 8) 8-12

'Shottendane, Margate. Designed by Mr Thackeray Turner'.
*Country Life* 34; (suppl Nov 15) 7-11

'Wolverton Court, Stratford on Avon. Its Repair and
Enlargement by Mr Clough Williams-Ellis'.
*Country Life* 34; (suppl Nov 22) 7-11

'Point Hill, Rye and its Enlargement by Mr Reginald
Blomfield ARA.'
*Country Life* 34; (suppl Dec 6) 8-12

'Upton House, Cambridge. Designed by Mr A Winter Rose'.
*Country Life* 34; (suppl Dec 13) 36-40

'Woodside, Hook Heath, Surrey. Designed by Mr Arthur
Messer'.
*Country Life* 34; (suppl Dec 20) 7-8

'The Repair of Ancient Buildings'.
(Discussion of paper by WA Forsyth)
*Journal of the Royal Institute of British Architects* 21; 137

'A Leaden Bust of Queen Elizabeth'.
*Proceedings of the Society of Antiquaries of London* 25; 116

## — 1914 —

'Acklam Hall, Yorkshire. The Seat of Mr W H Hustler'.
*Country Life* 35; 342-350

'Stobhall, Perthshire. The Property of The Earl of Ancaster'.
*Country Life* 35; 738-744

'The Budget and Cottage Traditions'.
*Country Life* 35; 789-791

'Glamis Castle, Forfarshire. The Seat of the Earl of
Strathmore'.
*Country Life* 36; 196-204

'Hallingbury Place, Essex. The Residence of Mr Lacket
Agnew'.
*Country Life* 36; 390-396

'Notgrove Manor, Gloucestershire. The Seat of Mrs Cyril
Cunard'.
*Country Life* 36; 378-383

'The Rodin Gift'.
*Country Life* 36; 667-668

'A House at Long Wittenham, Berkshire. Designed by
Mr E Guy Dauber'.
*Country Life* 35; (suppl Jan 3) 7-11

'Two Squash Racket Courts'.
*Country Life* 35; (suppl Jan 17) 7-11

'The Cottage, Charlton, Oxon, and its Enlargement by
Mr Alan James'.
*Country Life* 35; (suppl Jan 24) 7-10

'Cornerlot, Hardelot, France. Designed by Mr Somerset'.
*Country Life* 35; (suppl Jan 31) 7-11

'The Orchard Farm, Broadway, and its Remodelling by
Mr A N Prentice'.
*Country Life* 35; (suppl Feb 14) 8-12

'The Road Farm, Churt. Its Repair and Enlargement by
Mr R Atkinson'.
*Country Life* 35; (suppl Feb 21) 7-10

'Red Cot, Blundellsands. Designed by Mr F Atkinson'.
*Country Life* 35; (suppl Feb 28) 8–11

'West End, Broadway, and its Remodelling by Mr C Bateman'.
*Country Life* 35; (suppl Mar 7) 7–11

'The Old Bell House, Linford, and its Repair by
Mr B Stallybrass'.
*Country Life* 35; (suppl Mar 14) 8–15

'Woodgate, Purley, Surrey, Designed by Mr H Gilford'.
*Country Life* 35; (suppl Mar 21) 7–8

'Drakestone, Stinchcombe, Glos. Designed by Mr O Milne'.
*Country Life* 35; (suppl Apr 11) 11–13

'Porters, Southend, Essex'.
*Country Life* 35; (suppl Apr 18) 9–12

'The Country Life National Competition for Cottage
Designs'.
*Country Life* 35; (suppl May 2) 9–14
35; (suppl May 9) 9–15
35; (suppl May 16) 7–12

'Eastham Grange, near Tenbury. Designed by Mr W Tapper'.
*Country Life* 35; (suppl May 23) 7–8

'Defects in Cottage Planning'.
*Country Life* 35; (suppl May 23) 11

'The Eliot Cottage Hospital and the Bradford Almshouses,
Hayward's Heath'.
*Country Life* 35; (suppl June 1) 7–11

'Cottage Designs'.
*Country Life* 35; (suppl June 13) 7–10

'The House at Chislehurst. Designed by Mr E J May'.
*Country Life* 35; (suppl June 20) 9–13

'Moss Garth, Portingscale, Keswick. Designed by
Mr W H Ward'.
*Country Life* 35; (suppl June 27) 7–8

'Elm Tree Farm, West Wittering, and its New Garden.
Designed by M W H Godfrey'.
*Country Life* 36; (suppl Aug 1) 9–10

'St John's Priory, Poling, Sussex, and its Enlargement by
Mr P M Johnston'.
*Country Life* 36; (suppl Aug 8) 7–8

'Bingles Farm, Lye Green, Sussex, and its Repair by Mr Melville
Seth Ward'.
*Country Life* 36; (suppl Dec 5) 11–14

'English Church Monuments'. (Discussion of a Paper by
James Williams)
*Journal of the Royal Institute of British Architects* 22; 231–232

'The Complete Building Accounts of the City Churches
(Parochial) Designed by Christopher Wren'. (lecture)
*Proceedings of the Society of Antiquaries of London* 27; 45–48

— 1915 —

'The Complete Building Accounts of the City Churches
(Parochial) Designed by Sir Christopher Wren'.
*Archaeologia* (Society of Antiquaries) 66; 1–60

'The Village Hall, Nettlebed'.
*Country Life* 37; 86–88

'Castle Stewart, Invernessshire and Craigston Castle,
Aberdeenshire'.
*Country Life* 37; 112–116

'Farfield Hall, Yorkshire. The Residence of Mr George
Douglas'.
*Country Life* 37; 240–244

'Heale House, Wiltshire. The Seat of The Hon Louis Greville'.
*Country Life* 37; 272–277

'Hanover Lodge, Regent's Park. The Residence of Vice-Admiral
Sir David Beatty KCB'.
*Country Life* 37; 590–600

'Buckland, Faringdon, Berkshire. The Seat of Sir Maurice
Fitzgerald Bart, Knight of Kerry, and of Lady Fitzgerald'.
*Country Life* 37; 662-669
37; 698-705

'Rounton Grange, Yorkshire. The Seat of Sir Hugh Bell Bart'.
*Country Life* 37; 906-912

'Mestrovic and the Spirit of Serbia'.
*Country Life* 38; 168-170

'Roehampton house, Surrey. One of Queen Mary's
Convalescent Auxiliary Hospitals'.
*Country Life* 38; 232-239

'Murthly Castle, Perthshire. The Seat of Mr Stewart-
Fotheringham'.
*Country Life* 38; 456-463

'Flete, Devonshire. The Seat of Lt-Col Francis Mildmay MP'.
*Country Life* 38; 680-688

'Godolphin House, Cornwall. The Property of The Duke of
Leeds'.
*Country Life* 38; 869-874

'Two Essex Farmhouses. Designed by Mr WW Scott-
Moncrieff'.
*Country Life* 37; (suppl Jan 30) 2-4

'The Malting House, Cambridge. Remodelled by Mr A Dunbar
Smith & Mr C Brewer'.
*Country Life* 37; (suppl Feb 13) 2-4

'Prettyman's, Edenbridge, and its Enlargement by
Mr C Bowles'.
*Country Life* 37; (suppl Mar 6) 2-4

'Little Court, Chorley Wood. Designed by Mr J D Coleridge'.
*Country Life* 37; (suppl Mar 27) 3-6

'Felden Barns, Bovingdon. Designed by Mr H P G Maule'.
*Country Life* 37; (suppl Apr 3) 2-6

'Marshway, Walberswick. Designed by Mr F Jennings'.
*Country Life* 37; (suppl May 1) 2-4

'Brockhampton Church, Herefordshire. Designed by Prof
W R Lethaby'.
*Country Life* 37; (suppl May 15) 2-4

'Mill Hill, Bransby, Yorks. Designed by Mr D Blow and
enlarged by Mr A Powell'.
*Country Life* 37; (suppl May 22) 2-6

'Duchy of Cornwall, Kennington Estate'.
*Country Life* 37; (suppl June 26) 2-8

'Wolmerwood, Matlow Common. Designed by Mr A Winter
Rose'.
*Country Life* 38; (suppl July 17) 2-4

'Black Charles, Underriver, Kent. Its Repair and
Enlargement'.
*Country Life* 38; (suppl Aug 7) 2-4

'Moor Park, Breconshire, and its Enlargement by
Mr H L Beckwith'.
*Country Life* 38; (suppl Sept 4) 2-4

'Feathercombe, Hambledon, Surrey. Designed by
Mr E Newton'.
*Country Life* 38; (suppl Oct 9) 2-6

'Furze Hill, Willersey, Glos. Designed by Mr J V Ball'.
*Country Life* 38; (suppl Oct 16) 2-4

'The Thatched Cottage, Byfleet, Surrey. Designed by
Mr G Blair Imrie'.
*Country Life* 38; (suppl Nov 13) 2-6

'Eighteenth Century Bath: The Pump Room'.
*Country Life* 38; (suppl Nov 20) 2-8

'Moon Green, Wittersham'.
*Country Life* 38; (suppl Nov 27) 2-4

'Blythe Court, Edgbaston. Designed by Mr Herbert Buckland'.
*Country Life* 38; (suppl Dec 4) 3-6

'Two Cambridge Colleges and the Housing Problem'.
*Country Life* 38; (suppl Dec 11) 2-6

'Maurice Johnson FSA and the Early Meetings of the Society'.
*Proceedings of the Society of Antiquaries of London* 28; 135-140

## — 1916 —

'Waterston Manor, Dorsetshire. The Residence of Captain
Gerald V Couter'.
*Country Life* 39; 208-214

'Buckland Abbey, Devonshire. The Seat of Sir Francis F Eliott-
Drake Bt'.
*Country Life* 39; 338-344

'Trelowarren, Cornwall. The Seat of the Rev Sir Vyell Vyvan
Bart'.
*Country Life* 39; 450-453

'The Chamberlain Monument in the Abbey'.
*Country Life* 39; 484-485

'Carclew, Cornwall. The Seat of Captain Tremayne'.
*Country Life* 39; 590-594

'The Architectural Debt to France. The Building of Westminster
Abbey'.
*Country Life* 39; 702-705

'Ayscoughfee Hall, Lincolnshire. The Property of the Town of
Spalding'.
*Country Life* 39; 730-735

'Kelburn Castle, Ayrshire. The Seat of Commander the Earl
of Glasgow RN'.
*Country Life* 40; 182-186

'Brahan Castle, Ross-Shire. The Seat of Col Stewart-MacKenzie
of Seaforth'.
*Country Life* 40; 210-211

'Brodie Castle, Morayshire. The Seat of The Brodie of
Brodie'.
*Country Life* 40; 238-241

'Bradninch Manor, Devon. The Residence of Mr A L Radford'.
*Country Life* 40; 322-328

'The Public House of the Future'.
*Country Life* 40; 329-330
40; 357-358

'Buscot Park, Berkshire. The Seat of Lord Faringdon'.
*Country Life* 40; 490-497

'Public School War Monuments'.
*Country Life* 40; 497-498

'Canons Park. The Middlesex Residence of Sir Arthur du Cros Bart'.
*Country Life* 40; 518-526

'The Late Lord Kitchener's Hobbies'.
*Country Life* 40; 573

'The Generalife, Granada'.
*Country Life* 40; 734-741

'Stone Edge, Leek Wootton, Warwickshire. Designed by Mr H Bulkeley Creswell'.
*Country Life* 39; (suppl Jan 15) 2-4

'Comarques, Thorpe-le-Sohen. Remodelled by Mr E A Richards'.
*Country Life* 39; (suppl Feb 5) 2-4

'The Cob Cottage in Wiltshire. Designed by Mr D Blow'.
*Country Life* 39; (suppl Feb 12) 2-4

'An Account of Our Stewardship'.
*Country Life* 39; (suppl Mar 4) 3-9

'Cottages at Fabianki, near Wloclawck, Poland. Designed by Mr A E Gurney'.
*Country Life* 39; (suppl Mar 25) 2-4

'Lennoxwood, Windlesham. Designed by the Late C E Mallows'.
*Country Life* 39; (suppl Apr 8) 2-4

'The Golf House, Denham, Bucks. Designed by
Mr M Seth-Ward'.
*Country Life* 39; (suppl Apr 29) 2-4

'A Swedish Country House: Berga'.
*Country Life* 39; (suppl May 20) 2-6

'Kimbers, Haslemere. Designed by Mr A Chandler'.
*Country Life* 39; (suppl May 27) 2-4

'Ryman's Tower, Apuldram, Sussex, and its Remodelling by
Mr W Godfrey'.
*Country Life* 39; (suppl Jun 3) 16-20

'Kerfield House, Ollerton, Cheshire, and its Remodelling by
Mr P Worthington'.
*Country Life* 39; (suppl June 24) 2-6

'Exhibition of War Memorial Design'.
*Country Life* 40; (suppl July 22) 2-8

'Wittersham House, Kent, and its Remodelling by
Mr Lutyens'.
*Country Life* 40; (suppl Oct 7) 2-6

'A Wayside Inn in Essex'.
*Country Life* 40; (suppl Oct 14) 16-18

'A Row of Cottages at Preston, Herts. Designed by
Mr Lutyens'.
*Country Life* 40; (suppl Nov 4) 6-8

'Frank Sydney Chesterton'. (obituary)
*Journal of the Royal Institute of British Architects* 24; 45-46


— 1917 —

'What Architects Have Done in the War'.
*Country Life* 41; 19-21

'Manderston, Berwickshire. The Seat of the Hon Lady
Miller'.
*Country Life* 41; 60-64

'Newhailes, Midlothian. The Seat of Lt-Col Sir David
Dalrymple Bt RN'.
*Country Life* 42; 228-232

'Thornfield, Hampstead Garden Suburb. Designed by
Mr Cyril Farey'.
*Country Life* 41; (suppl Jan 13) 2-4

'High Chimneys, Windlesham. Designed by the Late
C E Marlows'.
*Country Life* 41; (suppl Feb 10) 2-4

'Houses on Lord Leigh's Estate. Designed by Mr H W Hobbiss
and Mr S Jones'.
*Country Life* 41; (suppl Feb 17) 2-6

'Little Offley, Herts, and its Reparation by Messrs Lucas and
Lodge'.
*Country Life* 41; (suppl Feb 24) 2-6

'Windyridge, Hampstead Garden Suburb, Designed by
Mr Flemming-Williams'.
*Country Life* 41; (suppl Mar 3) 2-4

'Hill End, Preston, Herts. Designed by Mr Lutyens'.
*Country Life* 41; (suppl Mar 31) 10-14

'The Michaelis Gallery, Cape Town. Remodelled by
Mr J M Solomon'.
*Country Life* 41; (suppl Apr 14) 2-6

'Selwood, Ealing. Designed by Mr P Morley Horder'.
*Country Life* 41; (suppl Apr 21) 2-4

'Hilltop, Sunningdale. Designed by Mr A E Richardson'.
*Country Life* 41; (suppl Apr 28) 2-6

'Bridgefoot, Iver, Bucks'.
*Country Life* 41; (suppl May 19) 2-6

'Hutchins Barn, Beaconsfield. Designed by Mr M Seth Ward'.
*Country Life* 41; (suppl May 26) 2-4

'Frithwood House, Northwood. Designed by
Mr M Macartney'.
*Country Life* 41; (suppl June 6) 2-4

'The Cloisters, Regent's Park. Designed by Mr M H Baillie Scott'.
*Country Life* 41; (suppl June 23) 14–18

'Amersfort, Berkhamstead. Designed by the Late Mr E Wilmot'.
*Country Life* 42; (suppl Sept 22) 2–4

'Memorials and Monuments'. (lectures)
*Journal of the Royal Society of Arts* 65; 817–822
65; 832–839
65; 846–851

## — 1918 —

'Report of Supplies Division', in *Report of Director-General of Food Production*
His Majesty's Stationery Office. London; 31–40

## — 1919 —

'Heywood, Ballinakill, Queen's County, Ireland. The Seat of Sir W Hutcheson Poe Bart.'
*Country Life* 45; 16–22
45; 42–47

'Westminster Abbey and Major Pawley
*The Outlook* 43; 395

## — 1920 —

'The Mistress Art'.
*The Outlook* 45; 117–118

'Bentley's Cathedral'.
*The Outlook* 45; 501–502

'War Memorial Inscriptions'.
*The Outlook* 46; 109

'Forgotten Surnames'.
*The Outlook* 46; 253

'The Art of A E Richards'.
*The Outlook* 46; 613

'Tasters of Literature'.
*The Outlook* 46; 638–639

## — 1921 —

'Discoveries at Amesbury'.
*The Antiquaries Journal* 1; 125–130

'Land Settlement Building Work of the Ministry of
Agriculture and Fisheries'.
*The Architects' Journal* 53; 460–461

'The Land Settlement Building Work of the Ministry of
Agriculture and Fisheries'.
*The Builder* 70; 432–433

'Rural Housing'. (lecture)
*The Builder* 71; 650

'The Old Common Field System'. (letter)
*Country Life* 49; 53

'The Land Settlement Building Work of the Ministry of
Agriculture and Fisheries'.
*Journal of the Royal Institute of British Architects* 28; 309–325

## — 1922 —

'Domestic Architecture'. (lecture)
*The Builder* 72; 236

'Modern Domestic Architecture'.
*The Builder* 72; 694

'Rural Settlement and its Relation to Public Health'. (lecture)
*The Builder* 72; 772

## — 1923 —

'Twenty years of British Architecture'.
*The Architectural Review* 53; 135

'The Gothenburg Exhibition'.
*The Architectural Review* 54; 201–207

'Small Holdings in the Future'.
*Country Life* 54; 62

'Getting Rid of the Basement'.
*Country Life* 54; 217–220

'An Antiquary in Languedoc'.
*Country Life* 54; 624–625

## — 1924 —

'Queen's Dolls' House'.
*The Architectural Review* 55; 82–85

'Exhibitors' Architecture'.
*The Architectural Review* 55; 222–229

'Domestic Architecture in England'. (lecture)
*The Builder* 77; 689

'Modern Room Decoration.
Winning Award in Country Life Competition Judged by
E L Lutyens, E G Woolrich, L Weaver, P Morley Horder,
N Wilkinson'.
*Country Life* 55; 46–48

'The National Theatre Competition.
Winner judged by J A Gotch, Sir E Lutyens, Sir L Weaver,
Mr H Granville-Barker, Prof C H Reilly, Prof H
Worthington'.
*Country Life* 55; 1017–1018

'Agriculture and Horticulture at the British Empire Exhibition'.
*Journal of the Ministry of Agriculture* 21; 9–14

'Exhibition of Modern British Architecture at the British
Empire Exhibition: Opening Ceremony'.
*Journal of the Royal Institute of British Architects* 31; 505–506

## — 1925 —

'The Topiarist at Home'. (book review)
*The Architectural Review* 58; 208

'Small Country House Competition.
Assessor's Award with a Criticism of the Designs by the Jury
of Sir Lawrence Weaver, Mr Leslie Mansfield, Mr P Morley
Horder, Mr Clough Williams-Ellis & Sir E Lutyens'.
*Country Life* 57; 409–416

'Subsidy Cottages at Wembley'.
*Country Life* 58; 112–114
58; 147–148

'Some Small-Holders' Cottages'.
*Country Life* 58; 645–647

'Cottages at Earswick'.
*Country Life* 58; 680–681

'Some Houses at Welwyn Garden City'.
*Country Life* 58; 835–836

'The Institute, 1917–1924 — A Retrospect'.
*Journal of National Institute of Agricultural Botany* 1; 51–57

'Modern Art in Industry: Lessons from the Paris Exhibition'.
(letter)
*The Times* (Oct 3) 6

## — 1926 —

'Modern British Craftsmanship'.
*The Architectural Review* 59; 122–123

'The Stockholm City Hall'.
*Country Life* 60; 769–771

'Ashtead Potters'.
*Rural Industries* 5; 2–3

## — 1927 —

'A Lesson from Sweden'.
*Design and Industries Association Quarterly Journal* 1; 4–5

## — 1928 —

'Tradition and Modernity in Craftsmanship.
I Plasterwork'.
*The Architectural Review* 63; 77-79

'Tradition and Modernity in Craftsmanship.
II Furnishing and Shopfitting'.
*The Architectural Review* 63; 247-249

'Tradition and Modernity in Craftsmanship.
III Metalwork'.
*The Architectural Review* 64; 119-121

'The Place of Advertising in Industry'.
*Quarterly Review* 250; 113-127

'Opening of Exhibition and New Sale Rooms at Country
Industries Ltd'. (lecture)
*Rural Industries* 13; 3-5

## — 1929 —

'The Architect as Accountant'.
*Architect and Building News* 122; 531-534

'English Chairs: Some Points in Anatomy'.
*The Architects' Journal* 69; 138-143

'Tradition and Modernity in Craftsmanship.
IV Furniture at High Wycombe'.
*The Architectural Review* 65; 48-50

'Tradition and Modernity in Craftsmanship.
V The Design of Gas Fires and their Settings'.
*The Architectural Review* 65; 99-104

'Tradition and Modernity in Craftsmanship.
VI A Study in Laminated Board'.
*The Architectural Review* 66; 252-258

'Stowe School Chapel'.
*Country Life* 66; 75-77

**— 1930 —**

'Laminated Board. Some Practical Details of the New Material'.
*The Architects' Journal* 71; 133-137

'The Man of the World'.
*The Architectural Review* 67; 226-227

'Art in Industry and Commerce '.
*Journal of the National Society of Art Masters* 2; 4-9